From the Corners of the Earth

Sunrise Hallel *service, Shavuot.*

FROM THE CORNERS OF THE EARTH

contemporary
photographs of
the Jewish world

BILL ARON

Introduction by CHAIM POTOK

The Jewish Publication Society
Philadelphia · New York · Jerusalem
5746 · 1985

TO THE MEMORY OF MY PARENTS

SAMUEL AND EVA ARON

and

TO ISA

Copyright © 1985 by Bill Aron
All rights reserved
Manufactured in the United States of America
Library of Congress Cataloging in Publication Data
Aron, Bill.
   From the corners of the earth.

   1. Jews—Pictorial works. I. Title.
DS108.5.A78   1985   909'.049240827   85–17185
ISBN 0–8276–0254–5 (paperback)
      0–8276–0276–6 (hardcover)

ACKNOWLEDGMENTS

Most people think of photography as an isolated artistic endeavor. My own work, however, has been deeply influenced by colleagues, mentors, and friends. Some gave me access to worlds that might never have admitted me; some contributed ideas, advice, or critiques; others lent me moral and financial support. I would like to offer my deepest thanks to: Isa Aron, Misha Avramoff, Roslyn Banish, Howard Becker, Nancy Berman, Richard Bryant, Shirley Burden, Paul Cowan, Gail Dorph, Shifra Epstein, Leonard Fein, Issica Gaon, Susan Goodman, Hayim Goldgrabber, Alice Greenwald, Grace Grossman, Irv Hahn, Sylvia Herskowitz, Greg Holmes, Michael Jacques, Barbara Kamilar, Elli Katzenstein, Carol Kur, Deborah Lipstadt, Riv-Ellen Prell, Morton Millman, Minolta Camera Co., Barbara Myerhoff, Bill Novak, Bernie and Sue Pucker, Sy Rubin, Dave Ruttenberg, Charles Sarner, Ahavia Scheindlin, Adele Schwarz, Richard Siegel, Yitzhak Zeev, The Jewish Community Foundation of the Jewish Federation Council of Los Angeles, and the clients and staff of Project Ezra on New York's Lower East Side.

I would also like to thank my editors, David Rosenberg and Barbara Spector, and the designer, Adrianne Onderdonk Dudden, who patiently sifted through my pictures and my words and gave the book its final form.

Lastly, and most importantly, I would like to thank the many people who over the years have allowed me to enter their lives and, in some cases, to invade their privacy. Not all of them appear on these pages, but all deserve my deepest appreciation.

Contents

Introduction
CHAIM POTOK

There is a story about Kafka and cameras. Two automatic photographic machines were installed in Prague in the spring of 1921. Informed of the machines and advised that the camera cannot lie, Kafka is reported to have remarked:

"Who told you that? Photography concentrates one's eye on the superficial. For that reason it obscures the hidden life which glimmers through the outlines of things like a play of light and shade. One can't catch that even with the sharpest lens. One has to grope for it by feeling."

In the matter of photography, Kafka, in Kafka-esque fashion, was both right and wrong.

The photographer who brushes his lens across the surfaces of things merely to record places and events is simply a bookkeeper. In such hands the camera is like the pen of an accountant or the register of a cashier: a tool that goes largely unnoticed as it dumbly accompanies the activities of man. It is said that we can never truly know a person or a thing from a photograph. To know an object is to understand it in its manifold relationships, to view it in a landscape of time, to perceive it as a story. A camera freezes an object; a narrative opens it, enters it, and reveals its pulsing heart. And so, in one regard, Kafka was right.

And yet he was not entirely right. For there are photographers who are like ice-axes, whose eyes are able to penetrate immediately to the fleeting moments of feeling and truth revealed even by the surfaces of the world: the swift gesture of a hand, the brief curl of a lip, the sudden tilt of a head, the flaring light in an eye— the flash of transcendence in the quotidian. To these photographers, nature and man yield up a universe of hidden life: serene nature watching indifferently the grim struggles of man gives us irony and beauty and truths we have still to come to terms with; man in endless striving offers us opportunities for dreams, for sympathy, for rage, contempt, love, and a sense of stoic endurance. In such instances, the automatic machinery of the camera appears linked to the biological eyes of the photographer—and the lens records not only the superficialities of things but also the poetry that lies both upon and beneath the surface, the nuances and concealed life that are the real truths of our world.

It seems to me that Bill Aron is such a photographer: a visionary with a camera, a recorder of the glimmers of light and shade that Kafka spoke about. Indeed, Aron uses his feelings to search for that obscured hidden life. In his hands a peripheral form, photography, seeks out the unseen—and becomes art. Aron waits with infinite patience for the revelatory moment, the odd juxtaposition, the sudden conjunction of disparate elements that create the possibilities for art. He does not impose the moment upon the object to force the surface into a simulation of art; there is no kitsch here. He lets the object itself unveil its own truth in its own good time. There is sympathy here, without sentimentality; a joy in artistic design, without glitz; the pain of truth, without the dubious palliatives of false assurances; a passion for human possibilities without a denial of the horrors we daily inflict upon one another.

To experience the fruit of Bill Aron's lens is to sense both the link to the divine and the infinite loneliness that constitute the essence of man. Kafka would have had much to contemplate had he seen the photographs in this collection.

Paris
June 1985

To 16th Street.

New York

The Lower East Side Revisited · 1974–1984

The Lower East Side of New York City is an important landmark in the life of the American Jew. It was, in its time, the source of a variety of Jewish cultural institutions: *yeshivot,* synagogues, Yiddish newspapers and theaters, as well as the restaurants and coffee houses depicted in the stories of Isaac Bashevis Singer.

The Lower East Side was one of the principal areas of settlement for Jews as they immigrated to this country. By the turn of the century it contained the largest Jewish community in the world.

In its heyday, East Broadway was a kind of Jewish promenade where a revered generation of artists, entertainers, politicians, businessmen, and intellectuals flourished. The neighborhood was bustling and vibrant, full of immigrants from many lands working to attain the American dream, or, at least, hoping that their children would. The whole range of Jewish life could be found there, from the pious Hasidim to the socialist Bundists, from the artists and scholars to the entrepreneurs.

For many Jews, however, the Lower East Side was only a stopping place. Financial success was usually followed by a move away from the old neighborhood. Irving Berlin, Eddie Cantor, Jimmy Durante, Jacob Javits, and David Sarnoff are but a few of those who came out of the Lower East Side. They started here, and when they began to "make it," they left.

The neighborhood that remains bears testimony to the struggle of that first generation of Jewish immigrants. Hundred-year-old tenements still stand with their shabby ornaments and fire escapes. Practically every doorway shows the signs of a former mezuzah. On nearly every block stands the remains of at least one synagogue, many of them only shells of their former selves.

There is Seward Park, the place where thousands of Jewish workers celebrated May Day. Across the street from the park stands the old *Forward* building, once the home of the large Yiddish daily newspaper. Pushcarts with knishes and kosher food can still be found. People still come from all over the city to shop on Orchard Street and to buy religious articles, also stopping off for a supply of Gus' extra sour pickles before returning home.

The ethnic composition of the Lower East Side is changing. Although the once-populous Jewish community is but a fraction of its former size, a young modern Orthodox community has been slowly growing in the area around East Broadway. Several synagogues have been renovated in an effort to attract and hold on to these new residents. The number of social services has increased, and street festivals have inspired a new pride in both the old and the new residents of the Lower East Side.

There are many elderly Jews who either remain on the Lower East Side from immigrant times or have recently returned. In spite of the obvious difficulties of their circumstances, the old people fight to survive—not just to stay alive but also to remain strong and independent. Their spirit and their dignity are an inspiration.

For better or for worse, these old Jews are wedded to their neighborhood and are determined to stay. In my photographs, I have tried to capture and preserve their community.

Orchard Street.

Orchard Street is just as it was fifty years ago, only the signs are now in English instead of Yiddish. Every Sunday the street is closed to traffic and there is a festival of bargains. It is also the time to haggle over prices.

Canal and Essex Streets.

Bargaining for fish.

There are no fixed prices on the Lower East Side;
that is, if you know how to bargain.

Scribe.

Every week while Rabbi Eisenbach was working on the scroll in this photograph, I would enter his store, ask questions about his work, and seek permission to take his picture. He always answered my questions but refused to grant permission for the photograph. On the first warm day of spring I happened to be leading a youth group on a tour of the Lower East Side. We stopped at Rabbi Eisenbach's door, which was open, and I explained as much of

the scribe's work as I could. As I was about to walk away, I saw the photograph that I wanted to take. My camera was around my neck, and so, with only the slightest hesitation, I took advantage of the situation. At one point, he raised his eyes over his glasses, then quickly looked back to his work. For several weeks afterward I was bothered by the incident. I finally made a print and took it to him, holding my breath, of course. He looked at it for a very long moment and then smiled and said, ''It's very nice. Thank you.''

Rabbi Eisenbach's son.

Sukkot.

Every year during the five days between Yom Kippur and Sukkot, a unique ''street festival'' is held on the Lower East Side. Instead of pottery, jewelry, and candles, the attractions are lulavim, etrogim, aravot, *and* hadasim, *the symbols of Sukkot. Canal Street, just off Essex Street, is lined with makeshift tables displaying the wares. Young boys loudly hawk ''aravot, hadasim, sheine aravot.'' Many stores, even those that usually sell appliances and cosmetics,*

are given over to the arbah minim. *Large signs proclaim the superior quality of their* etrogim *and* lulavim.

Prices are high at the beginning of the week. As the week progresses, however, prices fall. For the customers, the selection is dwindling; for the merchants, time is running out. The customers come from all over the New York area. All kinds of Jews come: Hasidic Rebbes and their followers, Orthodox Jews in narrow-brimmed hats, Israelis in crocheted kippot, *rabbinical students, even the rabbis of the Ethiopian-Hebrew Congregation in Harlem.*

The streets are lined with cars, double- and triple-parked; all receive parking tickets and no one seems to mind. Some people head straight for their favorite shops, where they buy with little hesitation. Some spend all day meandering around the area, carefully inspecting the merchandise, looking for the ''perfect set'' at the right price. And judging from the faces of those who have just made their purchases, apparently buying is even more fun than watching.

16

The Cheshinover Rebbe.

Hasidim always seem to have stepped out of another century. The Cheshinover Rebbe saw me photograph him as he crossed Canal and Essex Streets to buy lu-lavim and etrogim for Sukkot. He made no attempt to interfere with my photographing him, so I contin-ued to do so. After a while, one of his followers began yelling at me to go away. The rabbi cut him off gruffly, saying something in Yiddish. I surmised that I could continue. I later took his address and sent him copies of the photographs. After he received them, he called to thank me and to invite me to the wedding of a daughter of his brother-in-law, the Bobover Rebbe.

Tiferet Yerushalayim Yeshiva.

The library of the Pike Street Synagogue.

Hair tonic.

Our gang.

Henry Bookbinding Co.

The Muncasc Tallis Factory.

This is one of the oldest automated looms in the country. When I visit the loom, I can barely stay in the room for five minutes because of the clanging noises that the machine makes. The man in charge of the loom stays there for twenty to thirty minutes at a time. The fabric comes off the loom in large reams, which are then cut and basted. Afterward, the material is sent to a yeshiva in Brooklyn where, under strict rabbinical supervision, the fringes are tied on.

The oldest synagogue in New York.

Built in 1849 as Anshe Chesed, its present name is Anshe Slonim. In 1972, for the first time in a century, High Holiday services could not be held because the building was in such disrepair. A combination of deterioration and vandalism finally caused the synagogue to close its doors permanently in 1974.

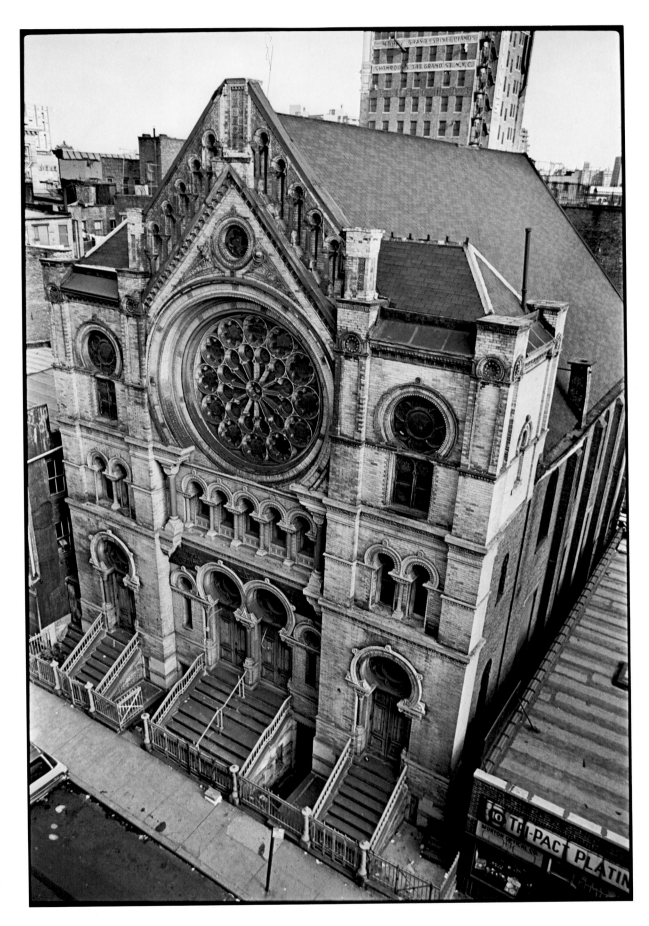

Eldridge Street Synagogue.

This is one of the most majestic synagogues on the Lower East Side. Although the building was intended to accommodate hundreds, today only a few come regularly to pray and study.

The Bobover Rebbe and granddaughter.

I was fortunate enough to be invited to the wedding of one of the daughters of the Bobover Rebbe. During the entertainment after the ceremony, this little girl broke away from the women's section and came running to her grandfather, who was, of course, delighted.

Wedding entertainment.

The battery-operated train at the top of the pole runs up the track and rings a bell when it enters the little house.

27

Hasidic bride.

Couple.

As I was photographing this couple, the husband
very spontaneously leaned over to kiss his wife.
''Here,'' he said, ''take this picture.'' I was so
taken by surprise, I had a difficult time getting the
camera set properly. But they held the pose.

The Upper West Side and the New York Havurah · 1974-1984

While living on the Upper West Side of New York, I was exceptionally fortunate to be a member of the New York Havurah, a group of young people committed to practicing Jewish traditions in new and alternative settings. The Havurah had no affiliations, either with a synagogue or with one of the movements within Judaism. Members were committed to traditional Judaism but were concerned with making it more democratic and egalitarian and less institution-bound.

During this period of my life, I was deeply involved with learning how to be Jewish, and, in addition, with using photography as a means of self-expression. A continuing frustration of mine is that often the most visually striking moments are those in which photography is either proscribed by Jewish law (by those who are observant) or considered disruptive. Ordinarily, therefore, I could not have found an outlet for combining my growing appreciation of Judaism with my need for making images.

Members of the New York Havurah, however, placed great importance both on self-expression and on the aesthetic dimension of Judaism. Probably because of this ethos, even members of the group who were extremely observant were tolerant of my taking pictures. They were conscious of the arts involved in the rituals and traditions they practiced and were proud to share and exhibit them through the medium of my photography.

The Havurah prayed together, studied together, and met for elaborate meals and long discussions. In addition, retreats were held outside the city one weekend every month and on special holidays. Two of its members conducted an afternoon school for neighborhood children. In all these activities, there was intensity, questioning, and intimacy, and there was also a great deal of fun.

The Havurah was one of the first groups I encountered that incorporated women as equal participants in ritual observance. Women served as Torah readers, cantors, discussion leaders, and teachers. They expressed their Judaism freely and totally, knowledgeably and capably. Because I was so struck by these positive images projected by the women in the Havurah, these women became the subjects of many of my photographs.

The principal strength of photography lies in its ability to give the viewer an emotional connection with the scene depicted. For me, the most meaningful and, visually, the most powerful aspect of Judaism is its rituals, which symbolically link the generations together. When I see the elements of a ritual act align themselves in some meaningful geometry, I want to make it last, to fix it permanently in a photograph. One of my greatest joys was having this freedom within the Havurah. Since 1978 I have been living in Los Angeles, and I feel that my life is just a little less fulfilling because there is no such group to tolerate my photographing religious moments.

Tashlich.

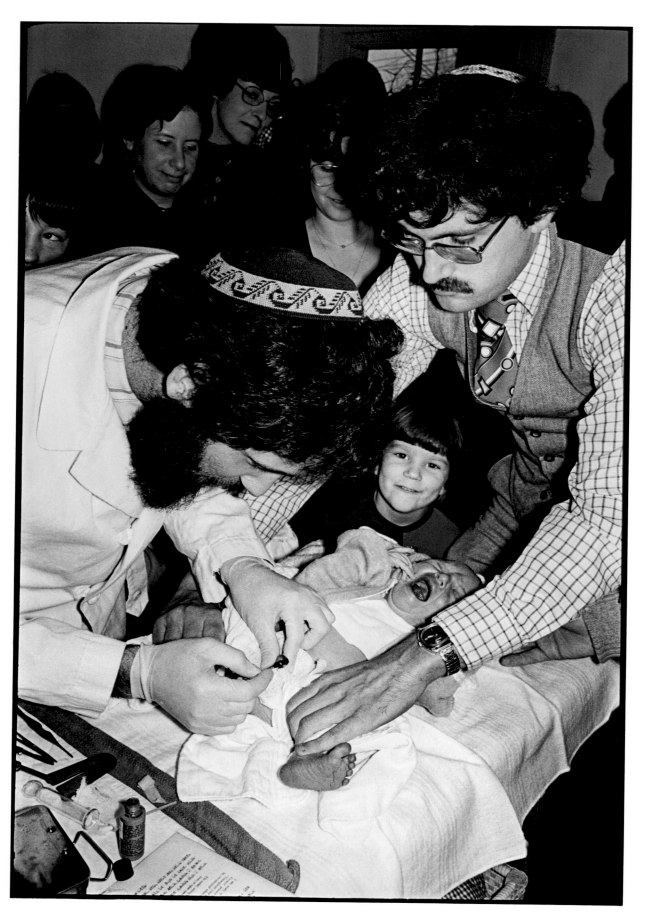

Brit Milah.

Simchat Torah.

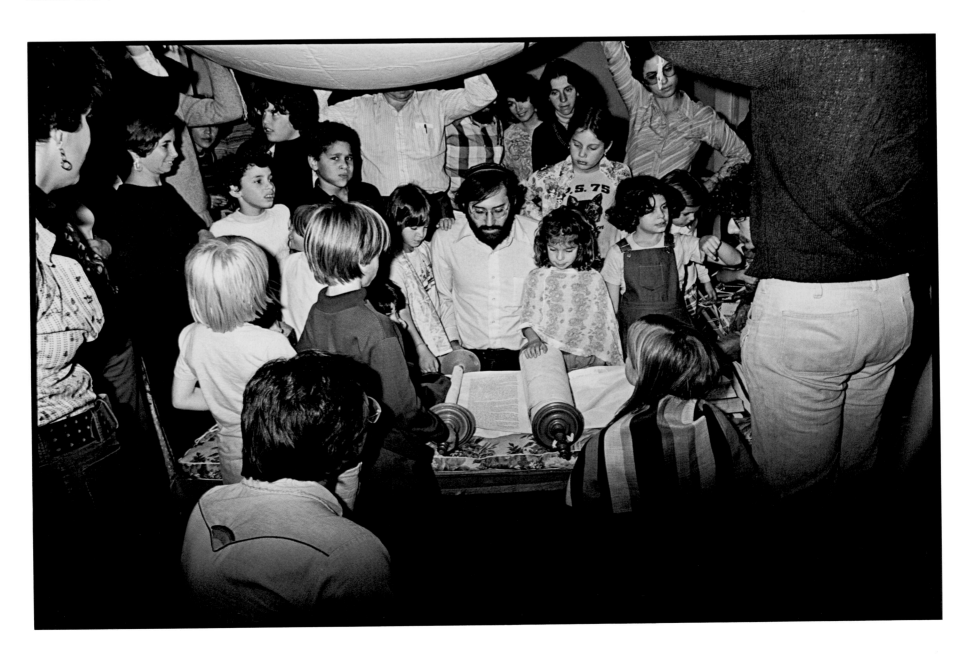

Simchat Torah.

Morning minyan.

Demonstration for Soviet Jewry.

36

Demonstration for Soviet Jewry.

Shavuot, Nyack, New York.

Sukkot, Connecticut.

Car, Los Angeles.

Los Angeles

Fairfax · 1980~1985

The Fairfax neighborhood consists of five square miles where approximately 32,000 people, most of whom are Jewish, live. Its name derives from Fairfax Avenue, which runs down its center and is the heart of Jewish Los Angeles.

Jews began moving into the Fairfax area in the 1930s from Boyle Heights, the principal Jewish area until that time. Between 1935 and 1945 about twelve synagogues, several religious schools, a *mikvah,* a number of Jewish social, political, and fund-raising organizations, and many kosher butchers, Jewish bakeries, and religious book stores were all established on Fairfax Avenue. The neighborhood became indelibly stamped with a Jewish character (some called it "The Kosher Canyon") and remains so today, some forty years later.

Jews still come from all over Los Angeles to shop in the stores of Fairfax, although most of what people come to Fairfax for can be found in other parts of the city. Jewish school children from the Valley are bused to Fairfax on field trips to see what a Jewish neighborhood is like. The Jewish Federation Council sponsors walking tours of the area.

The Jewish character of Fairfax still makes it an attractive area for new Jewish immigrants. During the 1960s, large numbers of Israelis began immigrating to Los Angeles and settling in Fairfax. Between 1960 and 1969, the Fairfax population grew by 25 per cent. The Los Angeles earthquake of 1970, which leveled Fairfax High School, caused many people to move out of the area. This was the only decline in population in the history of the Fairfax neighborhood (27 per cent decrease between 1970 and 1974). During the latter half of the 1970s, a large influx of Russian Jewish immigrants again swelled the numbers of Fairfax residents, this time by 60 per cent.

I live in the Fairfax area and I love it. I buy challah there. I run out and eat a felafel whenever I have the urge. I sometimes go to the storefront *minyan* that is held around the corner from my house. The Shabbat *minyan* I attend regularly is also less than a mile from my home.

Most of all, living in Fairfax anchors me in the past, something I find particularly comforting in this city. Los Angeles is a city of freeways and Hollywood glamour. It often seems as though its residents spend the majority of their time with machines: in their cars or in front of their computers, televisions, and VCRs. On Fairfax Avenue people still walk and use shopping carts. Young and old people mingle together in the stores as well as on the street. Russian, Hebrew, and Yiddish are more common than English. And some of the stores are forty years old, which, in Los Angeles, makes them landmarks.

Fairfax has a sense of the past, and that means that there is some continuity in life. Whenever the glitter of the Rolls Royces, the speed of the freeways, or the youthful appearance of everyone I see gets to be too much for me, I know I can always go to Fairfax, have a *glatt* kosher hot dog, and regain my equilibrium.

The late anthropologist Barbara Myerhoff, who in the last year of her life was engaged in making a film about the Fairfax area, spoke most eloquently about the neighborhood:

Fairfax is the kind of neighborhood that allows people to live together with humanity, dignity, and personal relationships, the kind that supports the frail, the elderly, the isolated and weaves them into the diverse fabric of commonality.

Here then is a neighborhood that is the hero of an important story. Community has been claimed to be in a state of deterioration in America. Not so in Fairfax: Here community is being actively sought and spontaneously regenerated by these Jews. This is no Melting Pot of Jews; on the contrary, diversity is more striking than ever, with new waves of immigrants pouring in from all over—Russian, Israeli, Middle Eastern. Fairfax is becoming known all over the Jewish world as a portal of entry, the new Ellis Island.

Fairfax and Oakwood bus stop.

Canter's Delicatessen and Bakery.

Fairfax Kosher Market.

Religious book and gift store.

Fairfax Sephardic Grocery.

Fairfax and Rosewood bus stop.

Barbara Myerhoff.

Polish immigrant.

Shalom Retirement Hotel.

Fairfax minyan.

Wedding band.

Interior of Breed Street Shul, Los Angeles' first synagogue. (This synagogue is located in Boyle Heights, another part of the city.)

Chabad Russian Synagogue.

Shabbat candles.

Jewish bakery.

Venice, California · 1979~1982

Approximately 4,000 elderly Jews live in Venice. Most immigrated to this country from Eastern Europe, pausing briefly on the East Coast and then continuing across America with California as their final destination.

Anthropologist Barbara Myerhoff, in *Number Our Days* (E. P. Dutton, 1979), characterized these people as survivors of a special kind. Despite their age, they are a politically organized and socially active population. They are passionate, full of pride, and independent, helping those they consider needier than they.

Many volunteer their time and services to other elderly groups throughout the city. They exercise regularly, often walking as much as 5 or 6 miles daily. For them, survival is a full-time occupation, and they work hard at it. They do whatever is necessary to remain as healthy as possible, whether that be a twice-daily swim in the ocean to combat arthritis or a dangerous operation to implant an experimental pacemaker.

In 1979, the Hebrew Union College Skirball Museum commissioned me to spend four months photographing the elderly Jews of Venice. During the course of the project, I found myself profoundly affected by their vitality. The forcefulness of their personalities was so engaging that I wanted to fill the viewfinder with them: with their hands, their faces, and their histories. I felt compelled, in most cases, to focus in on the life I found in these people, whose ages ranged from sixty-five to ninety-five. Nothing else seemed appropriate or important. I tried to make the photographs tell complete stories, as if the whole of their realities was within my viewfinder and looking at me.

These quotes from some of those I photographed reveal what I mean:

SAM: "As a youth, I lived in the face of the Russian Revolution. That spirit has moved me my entire life and colors everything I see."

SADIE: "I am a believer in the ecumenical outlook. We should all be friends. It's very important for us not to judge."

MINNIE: "I am entirely up on what's happening to seniors. The cuts the president is making are being borne by those that can least afford it."

BERTHA: "I have a lot of good friends, thank God, and people who know me and know who I am. But some of the people don't realize (who I am)."

PAULINE: "He said, 'Would you fight for your country if you become a citizen?' I said, 'I believe in peace.' 'Oh no,' he said, 'that's not what a citizen would say.' "

Gypsy.

Born in Lithuania, 1910. Came to the United States in 1930 and to the Los Angeles area in 1949. Gypsy was a nightclub entertainer and, over the years, assembled a large manikin collection.

Victor and Benjamin.

*Victor: Born in Russia, 1891. Came to the United
States in 1906 and to the Los Angeles area in 1936.
Benjamin: Born in Poland, 1904. Came to the
United States in 1923 and to the Los Angeles area
in 1976.*

Pauline and Max.

Pauline: Born in Rumania, 1900. Came to the United States in 1921 and to the Los Angeles area in 1941. Max: Born in Russia, 1893. Came to the *United States in 1913 and to the Los Angeles area in 1941. They were married in 1921. Pauline was a practical nurse, and Max worked as a presser of clothes.*

Esther.

Born in Poland, 1901. Came to the United States in
1928 and to the Los Angeles area in 1929.

Anna.

Born in Russia, 1894. Came to the United States in 1908 and to the Los Angeles area in 1945.

Becky.

*Born in New York City in 1910; came to the Los
Angeles area in 1973.*

Pauline and Morris.

Pauline: Born in Russia, 1895. Came to the United States in 1910 and to the Los Angeles area in 1949.

Morris: Born in Russia, 1893. Came to the United States in 1900 and to the Los Angeles area in 1933. Pauline worked as a medical assistant, Morris in a department store.

Vera.

Information unavailable.

Celia.

Born in Russia; came to the United States when she was fifteen years old. She came to the Los Angeles area in 1938 and worked in a grocery store with her husband, a rabbi from Bialystok.

Yetta.

Born in Poland, 1895. Came to the United States in 1920 and to the Los Angeles area in 1933.

Ocean Front Walk.

The Reform synagogue.

The Union Hebrew Congregation, Cuba's first synagogue, was founded shortly after the turn of the century by American businessmen who spent much of their time in Cuba. Today, the temple is in an advanced state of decay. The structure consists only of a small office and a large sanctuary. The congre- *gation therefore cannot retreat to a smaller room and rent out the large hall to raise funds, as other congregations do. Services rarely attract a full* minyan. *In 1965, they stopped adding metal plaques to the* yahrzeit *wall; since then, they use cut pieces of file cards.*

Cuba · 1978

In May 1978 I traveled to Cuba as a member of a group of ten Jews invited by the Cuban government to visit its Jewish community.

In the years since Fidel Castro's revolution in 1959, the Jewish community of Cuba has declined from 15,000 to about 1,000. Most of Cuba's Jews now live in Havana, where there are five large synagogues, all with Shabbat services. Only two are used on a daily basis. Ten to fifteen people attend each of the Shabbat services. There are no rabbis.

The major problem is not antisemitism but the fact that the state discourages the practice of any religion: Protestant, Catholic, or Jewish. Church members have the same problem as religious Jews; anyone who attends religious services cannot belong to the Communist Party and is therefore not eligible for promotion at his or her place of employment. Promotions are also withheld if service in voluntary Sunday work brigades is not performed. And, since everyone has to work on Saturdays, one rarely sees young people in synagogue or church. Only the retired have the luxury of religious practice.

Every morning I would rise at about 5:30 and, together with another member of the group, would wander through the streets photographing. By 7:30, we would reach one of the two synagogues with a morning *minyan*, Adath Israel or Chevet Ahim. In both synagogues there was warm hospitality. When there was a Torah service, we were honored with *aliyot*. After services, the people always insisted that we share their breakfast of tea and bread. It was like any Jewish community in the world, but there were differences, too.

Chevet Ahim.

The synagogue is located on the second floor of a building in the old section of Havana. The congregation also runs a restaurant/bar, across the hall from the synagogue. It has pictures of Castro, of Weizmann, and of Herzl, and a Magen David shaped out of neon lights. Chevet Ahim is open daily as well as on Shabbat and holidays; there is not always a minyan, *but services are always held.*

Cecilia.

Union Hebrea Chevet Ahim is one of two Sephardic synagogues in Havana. After the Turkish revolution, a number of Jews came from Turkey to Cuba in the 1920s and started this congregation, which met on the second floor of a building in the old section of Havana.

When I first entered Chevet Ahim I asked, through a translator, where the people were originally from. When they answered "Turkey," I could barely contain my excitement. I had spent four years in Turkey for the U.S. Peace Corps and have a good command of the language. When I asked if anyone still spoke Turkish, I saw and felt an excitement that matched my own. "Of course, we remember our Turkish," said Cecilia. It was like finding long-lost family. My Turkish was a bit rusty, as was theirs, but what we lacked in fluency we more than made up in enthusiasm.

The caretaker of Chevet Ahim.

Amidah.

To my surprise, the presence of my camera caused no disruption. During the concluding paragraph of the Amidah *prayer, it is a Sephardic custom to wave in addition to bending to the left and right.*

Lighting candles in memory of those who were martyred.

One of the most meaningful experiences I had in Cuba occurred on Lag B'Omer. There is a Sephardic custom of lighting candles commemorating the sages on Lag B'Omer, which derives from the tradition of lighting bonfires outside the city of Safed. About a dozen Cubans and six Americans from our group were present at Chevet Ahim for their Lag B'Omer services. After the evening service, everyone gathered around the table of candles, placing money on the table in exchange for the honor of lighting a candle. When the candles were all lit, the Hacham approached the pulpit and began leading the group in song. Some people sang, some continued talking with their neighbors; at one point I counted six languages being spoken: Hebrew, Spanish, English, Yiddish, French, and Turkish. There was an almost tangible feeling of good will and community. Then something magical happened. The Hacham started singing Hatikvah, and by the third word everyone had jumped to his or her feet and the room was bursting with song. We were all mesmerized, lost in our own worlds, yet somehow transformed into one voice, one prayer.

The Hacham.

Responsibility for the religious affairs of the synagogue rests with one man. He is called the Hacham, "the wise man." This is a Sephardic office, just lower than that of "Rabbi." He sees to it that services start on time, that the proper prayers are said, and that "Amen" is said at all the correct times. He knows the community is winding down, and he feels the responsibility for maintaining the tradition on his shoulders.

*Torah service at Adath Israel, the Orthodox
Ashkenazic synagogue.*

The oldest member of Adath Israel.

Mr. Weinberg leaves his house every morning at 5:30 to arrive in synagogue in time for morning services.

Adath Israel.

In Adath Israel, the Orthodox Ashkenazic synagogue, preparations were under way to move to a smaller prayer room in the basement. When Jews visit Cuba, which doesn't happen all that often, this synagogue is usually overlooked. As a result, when I *first visited Adath Israel the people were not only curious as to why I was there, but also somewhat bewildered. I was welcomed and accepted, just the same, and during the course of my stay a gradual warmth and a few friendships developed.*

The community's kosher slaughterer.

Adath Israel's minyan.

Cemetery.

*There are two Jewish cemeteries, one Ashkenazic,
one Sephardic, located a good distance from
Havana.*

The Sephardic cemetery.

Refusenik Isaac Kogan, Leningrad.
Electronics engineer. First applied: 1974.

His passion about Judaism, about the Torah, and about Israel has inspired scores of younger refuseniks in Leningrad.

The Soviet Union · 1981

By Spirit Alone: Soviet Jews Today

In the fall of 1981 I visited three cities in the Soviet Union: Leningrad, Minsk, and Moscow. My encounter with Jews there overwhelmed me with feelings: admiration, helplessness, anger, and compassion. I kept thinking that had my own father not emigrated when he did, I could be a Jew in the Soviet Union today. I wanted, therefore, to tell the story of the Jews with whom I met. I am a photographer, so I tell this story with my camera.

In each city I visited, I began by photographing in the synagogue. This is the common ground for the two groups of identified Jews in the Soviet Union: those who are trying to hold onto, or regain, their religious heritage, and those who wish to leave the Soviet Union—the refuseniks. The religious Jews, for the most part, are old, and the refuseniks are young. However, there are many obvious exceptions to this rule, and the two groups are by no means mutually exclusive. In recent years, especially, refuseniks have become more religious, and non-refusenik religious Jews have become more dissatisfied with their position in the Soviet Union.

My photographs, and my text, concern both these aspects of Russian Jewish life: religious and refusenik.

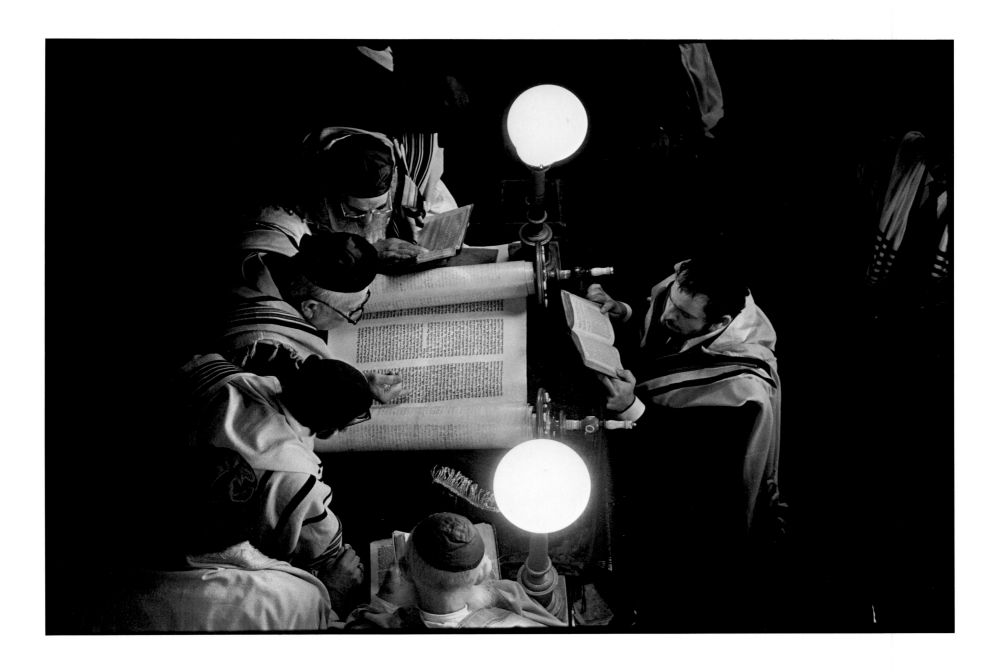

Yom Kippur Torah reading, Leningrad.

We arrived in the Soviet Union, in Leningrad, two days before Yom Kippur. The next morning we made contact with one of the refuseniks, who later escorted us to Kol Nidre services. When we rounded the corner where the synagogue was located, we were immediately enveloped by a large crowd of Jews. For a moment I stood there, not able to com- *prehend the reality of my surroundings. The feel, the smell, the sound, the very volume of the crowd all combined to suspend me, momentarily, in time. Memories of other Jewish experiences I have had whirled through my head: Jerusalem, Havana, New York, Los Angeles, and Chicago. Though I was in Russia, the land my father had left, I was also in all those other places.*

Gates to the Leningrad Synagogue.

Interior of Leningrad synagogue.

Kol Nidre, Leningrad.

After we pushed through the crowd into the synagogue, we made our way to the women's section. I sat next to an old woman who was reading her prayer book with a magnifying glass. I instinctively reached for my camera, and then froze. Since it was Kol Nidre evening, I wondered if the Russian Jews were going to object to my photographing on a holy day. I had been so worried about whether the Soviet authorities would allow me into the country with all my film and camera equipment, and whether they would interfere with my photographing, that I had not considered the feelings of the Jewish community. I quickly decided that my purpose in coming to the Soviet Union was to photograph, and if I held back, it would be a lost opportunity. So, with a great deal of anxiety, I began.

Indeed, there was some commotion as I took my first few pictures of the woman with the magnifying glass. Some in the congregation began to object to my photographing, but when they learned that I was an American visitor, their objections gave way to a desire to have their story told. One old man came up to me and said, ''Please, take my picture. Show my face. Tell everyone I am still here.''

Kol Nidre, Leningrad.

Hallel, *Sukkot, Minsk.*

One of the most moving experiences I had in the Soviet Union occurred in the Minsk synagogue, during the Hallel service on Sukkot. The man leading the prayers had been the first Hebrew teacher in Minsk. He used to sit in the synagogue, studying and teaching Hebrew to anyone who wanted to learn. One day in the early 1970s the KGB showed up, took him to their headquarters, and detained him overnight. When he returned to the synagogue he said nothing of the ordeal but was visibly shaken. He never gave another Hebrew lesson.

Sukkot, Minsk.

When this man chanted the Hallel prayers, every eye in the room was riveted on him. The emotion in his voice, the sincerity and strength of its sound, caused each note to seem to last forever. The silences between the notes were deafening. I could scarcely breathe; I was frozen by the fear of breaking the spell that filled the room. Not until the last few verses was I able to raise my camera and take a picture.

The synagogue and sukkah in Minsk.

Sukkah, Minsk.

On the first day of Sukkot, the old men of the Minsk synagogue shared their meager food with us in the sukkah. Their generosity, in spite of the obvious difficulty of their circumstances, overwhelmed me. It was the only time in the Soviet Union that I broke down. During our meal, amidst the singing, my eyes filled with tears. Lev Ovsischer, who was sitting alongside me, leaned over and said, ''Please don't. It is hard enough as it is.'' I had to leave the sukkah to recompose myself.

Sukkot, Minsk.

On the second day of Sukkot, we brought cake, bread, cognac, and chocolate (a luxury in the Soviet Union) to contribute to the meal after services. As we were about to enter the sukkah, the militia ar-rived, ostensibly to inspect the zoning permits for the new matzah-baking oven that was being built next to the synagogue. They said it would take a few hours, making it necessary, of course, to cancel the meal.

Old man, Minsk synagogue.

Moscow

Simchat Torah on Archipova Street in Moscow was an unforgettable experience. We arrived early, and already there were some 5,000 people in the street. We made our way inside the synagogue and upstairs with some difficulty. When we returned outside, we found about 20,000 Jews packed from one end of Archipova Street to the other.

Later that evening, the meaning of this mass experience became clear to me in the following story: "I have been secretly coming to Archipova Street on Simchat Torah for the last five years," said Boris, a middle-aged man. "It has been the one public way I have allowed myself to identify with the Jewish people. I never told other members of my family where I was going or what I was doing. I did not want them to worry, and I wanted no harm to befall them. This evening, as I made my way through the crowd, I came face to face with my eighteen-year-old son. Our eyes met in recognition. He had been secretly coming to Archipova Street on Simchat Torah for the last three years."

Simchat Torah eve, Moscow.

On the bimah, *Simchat Torah, Moscow Synagogue.*

Simchat Torah, Hakafot, *Moscow Synagogue.*

The Refuseniks

"What does it mean, 'being refused?' " Yuli
Kosharovsky once wrote in a letter. "This
means being dismissed from your job, to be
without money, to worry about your children
who are hounded in schools and who won't be
accepted in any institution, to lose almost all
your friends, to have trouble with the militia,
with house janitors, with neighbors and the
KGB. And this means that your time of life is
passing without return, that the present has lost
all sense and value, that you have been thrown
out of the present and not given a future, that
you are a shadow person."

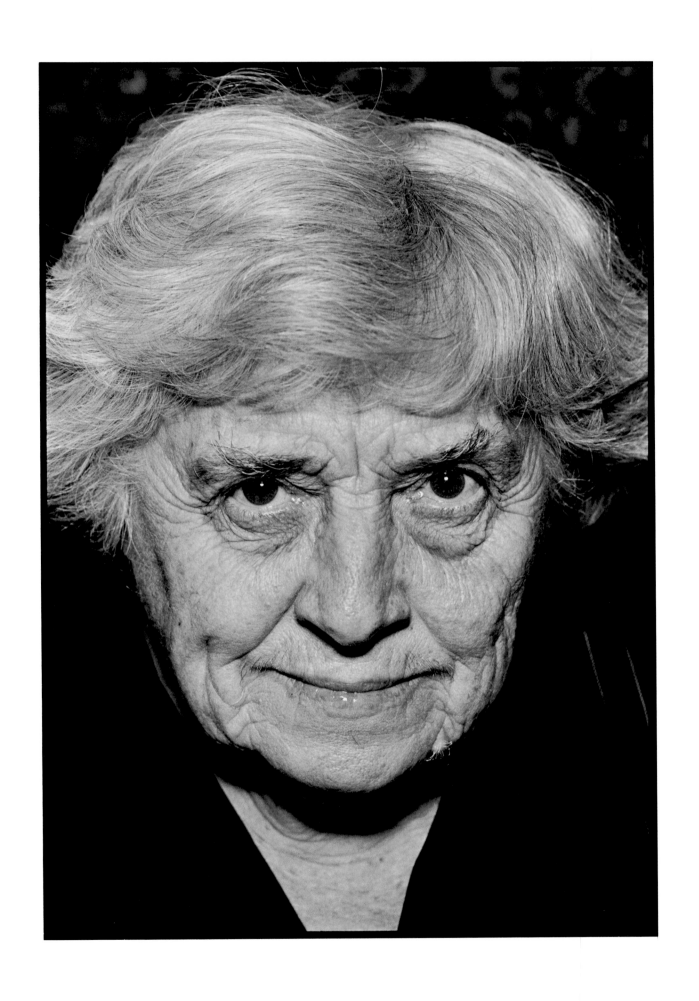

Ida Milgrom, Moscow. Mother of Anatoly Shcharansky.

Professor Aleksandr Lerner, Moscow. Cyberneticist.
First applied: 1971.

Retired Colonel Lev Ovsischer, Minsk.
First applied: 1972.

A retired colonel and a war hero, he says, ''What kinds of military secrets can a pilot who has been in retirement for sixteen years have these days?'' People say about Lev that he lives in three worlds. His heart is with his only daughter, who lives in Israel. His mind is with the refuseniks of Minsk, who study Hebrew and cherish Jewish culture, and his soul is with the old people of the synagogue.

Pavel Abramovitch, Moscow. Electronics engineer.
First applied: 1971.

*"The momentum of aliyah will only be maintained
in the face of hostility from the authorities if more
and more Jews understand their culture, their history, and their unbreakable ties with Israel and the
Hebrew language."*

Mara Abramovitch, Moscow. First applied: 1971.

Lev Blitshtein, Moscow.
Administrator in meat plant. First applied: 1974.

Lev is the former head of the meatpackers' union.
When his visa was refused, it was refused for rea-
sons of state security. When I asked him what could
be secret about packing meat, he said, ''Officially
it's how much meat there is in the Soviet Union—
unofficially, it's how little meat there is.'' And anec-
dotally, he likes to say that the secret is that he is
the only one in the Soviet Union who knows how to
make sausages without meat.

Genady Feldman.

Inna and Yuli Kosharovsky, Moscow.

"It's hardly the ideal way to plan a family, but we've been waiting seven long years, and life just has to go on however hard things are."

Michail Kosharovsky, Moscow.

"I often talk man-to-man with my son about our situation. I try to be constructive. When on the eighth anniversary of our first refusal, he asked me, 'Well, how long are we supposed to wait?' I felt ashamed. I had no answer to give him" (refusenik parent).

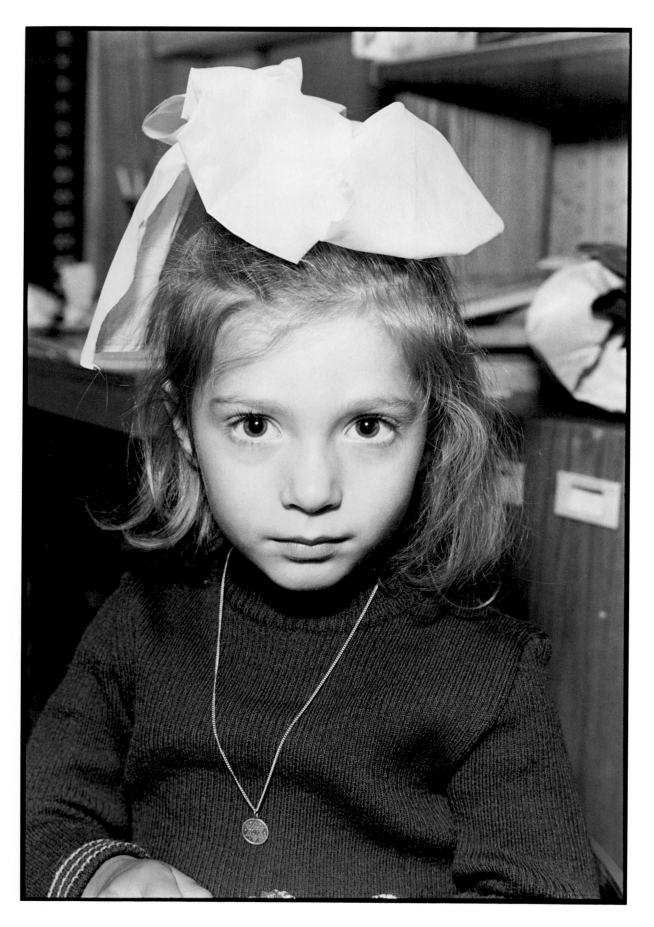

Alla Zeliger.

''Being a child refusenik is to suffer disappointment at second hand. They are the barometers of how things are with us. When our hopes are high, we see it in their faces, and when things are particularly difficult, we see our own anxiety reflected in them'' (refusenik parent).

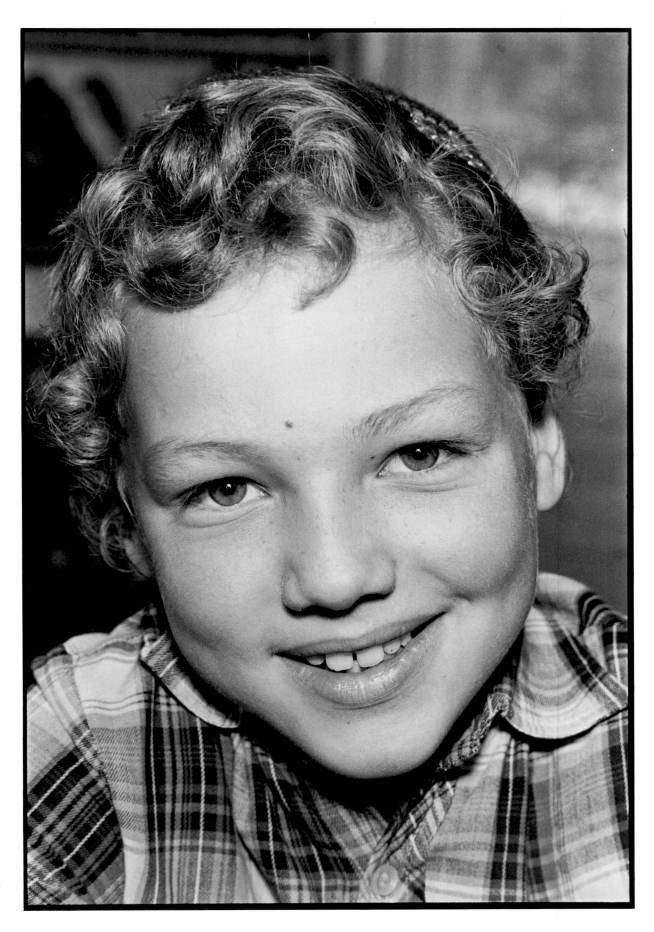

Ephraim Rosenshtein, Moscow.

"We Jews are a community based on memory. By denying us the right and ability to transmit our heritage to our children, Soviet authorities are bringing about the destruction of our most precious possession" (refusenik parent).

Rachel Genusov.

''Now we are here . . . next year, may we be free''
(Passover Haggadah).

Postscript

Many people have asked me if I had trouble photographing in the Soviet Union.

Although there was no direct interference, there were several incidents that made me realize Soviet authorities were concerned with my activities. In Minsk, my traveling companion, Ahavia Scheindlin, and I were called to the office of the local Intourist director (presumably KGB-affiliated) and warned that "The militia reported you were observed in the synagogue engaged in non-tourist activities." When questioned, he refused to specify, much to my relief, what those activities were. Thereafter, while in Minsk, Ahavia and I were constantly followed.

In addition, a week later in Moscow a rather official-looking man went out of his way to take our picture and then run away.

Anticipating that I would have trouble getting out of the country, I developed a plan to disguise my film. I took about twenty rolls of unused film and rolled them into their canisters. I labeled each canister with a provocative name, such as "document," "synagogue," "Jew," and "police." I put this decoy film in a plastic Baggie in my camera bag. I then put the real rolls of film back in the original canisters and tried to make them look unused. I packed that film in a lead bag in my regular suitcase.

Ahavia and I went to the airport as late as possible. As soon as we arrived at the Customs line we were whisked away to a separate section (we presumably were recognized from pictures taken by the mysterious Moscow photographer). Our bags were thoroughly searched; even each article of dirty clothing was inspected. When asked about the film in my suitcase, I explained that it rained a lot, so I didn't have a chance to use all the film I had brought with me.

When they went through my camera bag, I became visibly nervous. As soon as they found the (decoy) bag of film they separated it from the rest of my belongings. I screamed, yelled, jumped up and down, and generally made a fool of myself. I said they had no right to touch my personal property and I wanted the American Embassy called. The Customs officials, of course, only laughed and paid no attention to me. We were also taken to a private room, where our persons were searched. All our notes were taken, photocopied, and returned.

Our plane was delayed three to four hours to wait for us. The decoy film was never returned, and I protested about it the whole time. (I was so nervous it was about the only thought I could keep in my head.) Ahavia had made a tape recording of some music from the Yom Kippur service. That tape was also confiscated.

When we were finally released, the woman who escorted us to the plane was the last Russian official we saw. In the midst of my parting tantrum, she said to us, "At least you don't have to live here. You can leave."

After we boarded the plane, the BOAC stewardess told us not to relax until we were in the air. The previous month the plane was called back from the end of the runway so the authorities could question one of the passengers who had apparently had a similar experience to ours.

It wasn't until we arrived in London and received all our luggage, with the film, that we breathed easily.

Cat.

Jerusalem ·
1980

For many years I had thought about going to Jerusalem to photograph, but the timing was never right. One year, we had just moved to a new city. Another year, I was preparing for a major exhibition. Still another year, our first son had just been born. And so on. There was always an obstacle to my going to Jerusalem, even for a vacation.

Finally, the inevitable happened. My wife had to go to Israel for two months to attend professional conferences. Lacking a good excuse to stay home, I reluctantly agreed to the trip.

Once the decision was made, of course, the real reason for my procrastination became transparently clear. What could I possibly see that had not already been photographed a thousand times over? What could I possibly say photographically about a place where millions of photographs are taken every year—some of them by my heroes and mentors?

This fear and trepidation caused me to ignore the admonition I give my classes at the beginning of each semester. I talk about how every person has a distinct personality which, when combined with a set of skills, can produce a unique vision of the world. The challenge is learning to listen to, and trust, that inner feeling—our gut instinct, if you will—that can guide us in deciphering what is right and wrong, appropriate and inappropriate, good and bad, regardless of the endeavor.

Be that as it may, my family and I arrived in Jerusalem, settled into our apartment, and found a babysitter for our one-year-old son. I then set off with my assorted equipment (two camera bodies, three lenses, one hand-held light meter, and plenty of film) to explore the city.

Everywhere I walked, I was confronted by sights filled with contradictions: the intensity and brilliance of the sun versus the depth and darkness of the shadows; the comfort and familiarity of a homeland versus the strangeness and alienation of another culture; Shabbat at the Wall versus Shabbat at the swimming pool of the King David Hotel; the beauty of the land versus the omnipresence of the war.

There was much with which I had to come to terms. First, the light: Aside from the technical difficulty of capturing details within the shadows as well as within the bright highlights, I wanted to convey that special quality of Jerusalem's light—that feel of the light that both defines the city and is defined by it.

Second, Shabbat: I have often been criticized for photographing on Shabbat and other holidays. This is a difficult issue for me. On the one hand, some of the images that I witness are of such compelling beauty that I could not do otherwise than try to capture them. On the other hand, after I invade that space with my camera, the very essence of what had drawn me there is sometimes left disturbed. The struggle remains ongoing within me: the urge both to interpret the beauty that I see and to refrain from touching it.

Third, the landscape: Every stone in Jerusalem has a history that one feels while walking the streets. The conquerors, sages, even ordinary citizens have all left their mark. There were many places in Jerusalem that I grew fond of and to which I would return, sometimes on a daily basis, throughout the summer. I would continually search for some combination of light and circumstances that would make the ''right'' picture. Once in a while a particular situation would assert itself with a definite finality.

Lastly, something must be said about Jerusalem's people, its citizenry. Some Hasidim allowed me total freedom to photograph, some ''modern'' Jews objected to my presence; some adult Arabs welcomed me, some children threw stones; some families treated me as a member, others ignored or threatened me. No one lived up to his or her stereotype.

Each community I have photographed has presented a different set of challenges, both technical and emotional. The most taxing, however, was Jerusalem, because of its inherent symbolism. The necessity of working day to day to find new ways of seeing the everyday picturesque forced me to modify my way of photographing. Having confronted the anxieties and worked through the problems, I find, in retrospect, that the experience has enriched not only my feelings for Jerusalem, but also my photography.

Tallit *steps*.

Early morning Shabbat light.

King George, Jaffa, and Strauss Streets.

Mea Shearim.

Yeshiva student.

Laundry day in Jerusalem.

Hanging gartels.

School bus.

Shadows in the Old City.

Kasim Bey, a Turkish merchant.

On the way to the Wall.

Girl praying at the Wall.

Woman praying at the Wall.

The Wall.

Tisha B'Av at the Wall.

After prayers at the Wall.

Adin Steinsaltz.

The white donkey.

Olive trees.

Mount of Olives sunset.

Mount of Olives.

The army on patrol.

Mount of Olives.

The army on patrol.

The army at play.

About the Photographer

Bill Aron is a freelance photographer with a Ph.D. in sociology. He has shown his photographs in the Jewish Museum of New York, Hebrew Union College Skirball Museum, the Museum of the Diaspora in Tel Aviv, and the Museum of American Jewish History—among others. A wide variety of magazines and books using illustrations have been enriched by his work, including photo essays in *The Village Voice*, *Camera 35*, *Moment*, and *The National Jewish Monthly*. Bill Aron's images are in the permanent collections of museums in New York, Boston, Los Angeles, Philadelphia, Jerusalem, and Tel Aviv. He is represented by the Pucker/ Safrai Gallery in Boston and lives with his wife and two sons in Los Angeles, where he teaches Visual Anthropology at the University of Southern California.

This book was composed by N. K. Graphics using Meridien for the text type and ITC Isbell for the display type. The photographs were reproduced as duotones in 300 line screen on 80 lb. Warren's Lustro Offset Enamel. The book was printed by Meriden-Stinehour Press, bound by Publishers Book Bindery, and designed by Adrianne Onderdonk Dudden.